NOTE FROM THE AUTHOR

I want to personally welcome you to the Five Elements Manifesting Journal. I'm honored that you will allow me to take you on this journey to manifest your goals and dreams.

The Five Elements have been a personal guide for me in health, home, business, relationships, and creative projects. I was first introduced to the Five Elements through my practice as a feng shui consultant and later through my acupuncturist. It was through this overlapping use of the elements, both based in Taoism, when I understood how the Five Elements pervade everything in our lives here on earth.

In my book, *Missing Element, Hidden Strength*, I took the elements beyond feng shui to explore how the elements show up in our own energy and personality. Although we contain all five elements, we each have a primary element and what I call—your missing element. I have provided the quiz in the journal for you to explore these aspects of yourself and to discover your personal elemental constitution. This will be helpful as you progress through each step of the creative process, called the Five Elements Method.

The Five Elements Method will take you element by element through the creative process to create anything—a book, a podcast, a business idea, a yoga class, a relationship, an art project, really anything you have a desire to create or manifest.

The purpose of this journal is to use the Five Elements as a guide to manifest. By following my Five Elements Method in the pages that follow, you will have a step-by-step plan—part intuitive (yin), part analytic (yang) —to complete anything you set out to accomplish.

I wish you sweet dreams and abundant manifestations for your life and all those touched by your creations.

-Tisha Morris

HOW TO USE THIS JOURNAL

This journal contains pages for you to work through, explore, and manifest up to three goals or ideas. First, start with the Five Elements Quiz that is provided. This will show you how you rank among the elements and will be useful information for knowing which phases of the creative process come easy and those that are more challenging for you.

After you've journaled and reflected on your elemental constitution, familiarize yourself with the Five Elements Method, which lays out the Five Elements as five phases of the creative process. It is these five phases you will use to manifest your goal. But first you must write down your goals on the page provided, called GOALS. Use this journal for up to three goals—at once or used over time—as important goals come into your awareness.

You're also given space to explore your goal using a Tarot spread. This is optional and not necessary to manifest your goal. The traditional Tarot is made up of seventy-eight cards that represent the archetypes of the Hero's Journey*. They are also broken down into four elements which can be *loosely* translated to the Five Elements as shown here:

Pentacles = Earth
Swords = Metal/Wood
Hearts = Fire
Cups = Water

After your optional Tarot spread, it's time to start the Five Elements Method starting with Water and ending with Metal. Take the journaling prompts at a pace at comfortable for you. They are intended to be completed over time as as you work towards your goal and also for planning your next steps. With each goal, you'll move consecutively from the Water Element prompts followed by Wood Element, Fire Element, Earth Element, and the Metal Element prompts.

*A more thorough explanation of the Tarot is beyond the scope of this journal.

INTRODUCTION TO THE FIVE ELEMENTS

The process of creating something out of nothing is the manifestation process that we ourselves are all byproducts of and therefore embody within us. To create is to participate in the essence of being alive. This is what nature is busy doing all day too. All beings on earth are part of the creative process, which Taoism refer to as the Five Elements Cycle. The Five Elements Cycle is the interplay of the Five Elements—Water, Wood, Fire, Earth, and Metal—to create and sustain life on earth.

Taoism is an ancient eastern philosophy that sees the interrelationship of plants, animals, nature, human beings, and even inanimate objects as one with each being a microcosm of the Universe. The glue, so to speak, that ties all things together is the Five Elements. Everything consists of some combination of the Five Elements, including ourselves. Simultaneously, when the Five Elements work together in a cycle, they produce the creative cycle, also known as the manifestation process of turning thoughts into things.

When the Five Elements work together, they create a dynamic energy that is the creative process. To understand the process better, it's important to understand the role of each element individually. You can think of each element literally, metaphorically, or symbolically. For example, the Wood element includes what you would think of as wood, such as a tree, but it can also be represented energetically in a variety of ways, including a season, color, shape, and through our personality.

Let's look at how each element presents itself through our own personal energy and personality. As you take the Five Elements Quiz and read the element descriptions that follow, take note of your unique Five Elements Profile. We all contain the energy of all five elements, but we are usually dominant in one or two of them. Also notice if there is one of the elements that is definitely not you. It may hold the key to unlocking the manifestation process for yourself.

THE FIVE ELEMENTS QUIZ

For each statement, score yourself using the following:

2 = VERY MUCH LIKE ME

1 = SOMETIMES LIKE ME

0 = NOT ME AT ALL

Group A Questions:

_____ People would say I'm shy or quiet.

_____ I don't set goals because you never know where life will take you.

_____ I can easily get lost in my own world.

_____ I would rather stay at home with a good book than attend a social event.

_____ People don't really know me outside my inner-circle and I'm good with that.

_____ **Group A Score**

Group B Questions:

_____ I love starting new projects and often have multiple going at the same time.

_____ I'm often on the cutting edge in my work and love learning new things.

_____ I'm good at making decisions and take action on them rather quickly.

_____ People see me as a leader.

_____ I get frustrated when things don't happen fast enough.

_____ **Group B Score**

Group C Questions:

_____ I'm a better speaker than writer, but I enjoy all forms of communication.

_____ When I'm passionate about a project, I'm all in and can almost become obsessed with it.

_____ I am generally a people person and enjoy the company of others.

_____ I am affectionate.

_____ At times, I exhaust myself to the point of crashing.

_____ **Group C Score**

Group D Questions:

_____ I don't make a lot of changes, but when I do they're pretty major.

_____ In social or family groups, I tend to be the glue that keeps everyone together.

_____ I'm very supportive of other people's goals and will even go out of my way to help.

_____ I'm more likely to go along with the group rather than assert my opinion and upset people.

_____ My friends often lean on me for advice and support.

_____ **Group D Score**

Group E Questions:

_____ I tell people the truth without BS or embellishments.

_____ I maintain a neat and orderly environment without too much clutter.

_____ I am self-disciplined.

_____ I prefer an analytical approach to problem-solving rather than relying on feelings.

_____ I like to keep things organized.

_____ **Group E Score**

_____ GROUP A SCORE = WATER ELEMENT

_____ GROUP B SCORE = WOOD ELEMENT

_____ GROUP C SCORE = FIRE ELEMENT

_____ GROUP D SCORE = EARTH ELEMENT

_____ GROUP E SCORE = METAL ELEMENT

YOUR FIVE ELEMENTS PROFILE

From your scores above, make a list of your elements from highest score to lowest score. This is your personal Five Elements Profile. It's the energetic recipe that makes you *you*.

#1 _____← **Your Primary Element**

#2 _____

#3 _____

#4 _____

#5 _____← **Your Missing Element**

THE WATER ELEMENT

The Water Element is the Philosopher. They are quiet and typically introverted, and yet so unassuming. They hold a quiet strength. They may seem fragile at times, but they are anything but. They are deeply creative, contemplative, and introspective. They will most likely be the ones to figure out the key to world peace or an invention that saves climate change. It will be up to the other elements however to implement it. When out of balance, Water elements can become withdrawn and aloof. They tend to keep their emotions close to them and process slowly before taking action. In Taoism, the Water Element is associated with Winter.

THE WOOD ELEMENT

The Wood Element is the Pioneer. They are the leaders, inventors, seekers, and visionaries. They will take the lead in groups and take action steps to create movement in projects. They can easily vacillate between being introverted and extroverted depending on what a situation calls for. For example, they can work solo on creating a new business or work well with groups. When movement in projects or relationships stalls, the Wood element is quick to become frustrated. Wood elements keep things in forward motion and their challenge is to know when to contract their energy or take a step back. In Taoism, the Wood element is associated with Spring.

THE FIRE ELEMENT

The Fire Element is the Manifestor. They are high energy and generally extroverted. They are often the life of the party and enjoy life. Similar to a flame, they create the highest expression of energy in the form of enthusiasm and passion. Fire elements provide the fuel in projects in order that they manifest in its highest and truest form.

While the idea may have been born with the Water element, and the Wood element provided forward motion, it is the Fire element that brings something to full culmination. When out of balance, the Fire element can become burnt out. Its energy can easily scatter in too many areas without proper focus, which can lead to anxiety. In Taoism, the Fire element is associated with Summer.

THE EARTH ELEMENT

The Earth Element is the Stabilizer. They are the grounding force that keeps the status quo maintained so that change doesn't happen too quickly. The Earth element is the container or stage on which we all get to play. They are highly supportive people that bring harmony to groups and help maintain the peace. Think of the Earth element as the parent that keeps harmony among the children when bickering ensues. They go out of their way to not ruffle feathers. They do not like change and can become controlling if taken to the extreme. Worry is their default emotion, especially when something seems out of their control that could lead to possible change. In Taoism, the Earth element is associated with the equinox points.

THE METAL ELEMENT

The Metal Element is the Organizer. They are natural organizers and keep things in check and on schedule. They make great accountants, engineers, scientists, editors, architects, personal assistants, and professional organizers. They are guaranteed to be detail-oriented, focused, and precise in anything they do. They tend to cut to the chase in conversation without the need for embellishments. They also love an orderly environment with even their storage items labeled appropriately. Their imbalance can show up as being obsessive, perfectionist, or overly rigid in their mindsets. They tend to have tunnel vision without the ability to see a bigger picture. In Taoism, the Metal element is associated with autumn.

REFLECTIONS ON YOUR FIVE ELEMENT PROFILE:

PRIMARY ELEMENT:

MISSING ELEMENT:

THE FIVE ELEMENTS METHOD

The Five Elements can be used as a template for completing any creative project. For my example, I will use it for completing a book. For any project, however, it can be helpful in not getting overwhelmed with the process. As I take you step-by-step through my example using the Five Elements as my guide, know that this same process can be used for completing anything you set your mind to.

Like all things creative, a book starts with an idea. The idea phase is the Water phase, where thoughts and ideas drop in seemingly out of thin air. It's the phase in which the veils are the thinnest and you can be a channel from spirit. Everyone's process for how this happens differ. For example, some people get ideas through meditation, walking in nature, or during dreaming at night. Our best ideas often come when we're not trying to think about them because they come from beyond our physical brain.

The Water phase is also associated with knowing your *why*. In other words, what's driving you to write about or explore a certain topic or story. Your why becomes the river that quietly flows underneath your project and takes you to the end. Your why will get you past the doubts and fears along the way. It may feel like your mission or purpose, or something bigger than yourself, because it's the element that's most closely linked to the spirit world.

When you're ready to put your idea onto paper or into your computer, you've officially entered the Wood phase. The Wood phase is when we take the nonphysical idea into some physical form. In Taoism, it's represented by the first buds of spring making themselves visible in the natural world. You can think of it as the beginning of your idea blooming. This can take the form of an outline, the first pages, or simply jotting your ideas down in your journal. The Wood phase helps put structure to the otherwise invisible idea. You can think of it as a map that helps you plot your journey going forward. Once you've worked enough of your idea out on paper, then it's time to enter the Fire phase.

The Fire phase of any creative project is the phase in which you put in most of the work. In terms of writing a book, it's the bulk of the time it takes to actually write the book, or at least write the first draft. The Fire phase is represented by the summer season when the planting season is in full growth. It is in essence the highest point of energy output, which precedes harvest when the energy slows down. You can think of this as the completion of the first draft at which time you take a break from it. This is the Earth phase. It's the point of the creative process where you take an objective step back to reassess what you've created thus far.

After you've taken a break from your manuscript, it's time to start the editing phase. This is the Metal phase of the creative process where you go back to make any refinements needed. The energy of the Metal element is such that it cuts back or takes away any excess that may have occurred during the Fire phase. This phase is pertinent to any creative endeavor to finetune the final product. Whether creating a book, a product, or a new business, we are alchemists turning thoughts into things through the creative process of the Five Elements.

GOALS

GOAL #1

GOAL #2

GOAL #3

GOAL #1

FIVE ELEMENTS TAROT SPREAD

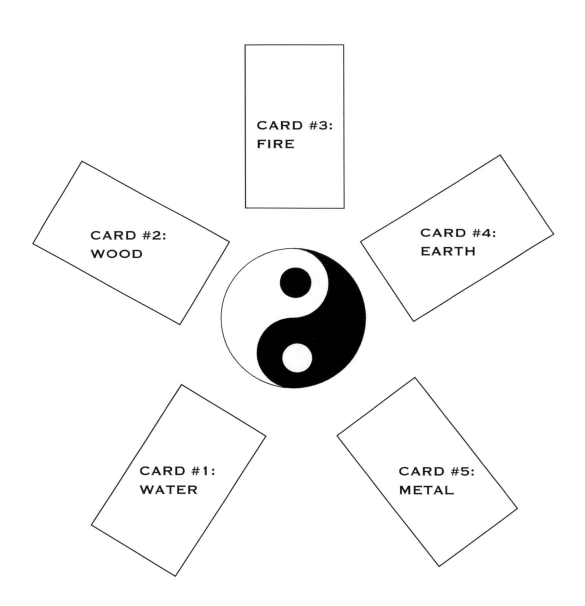

GOAL #1 TAROT NOTES

CARD #1 (WATER):

CARD #2 (WOOD):

CARD #3 (FIRE):

CARD #4 (EARTH):

CARD #5 (METAL):

ADDITIONAL NOTES:

GOAL #2
FIVE ELEMENTS TAROT SPREAD

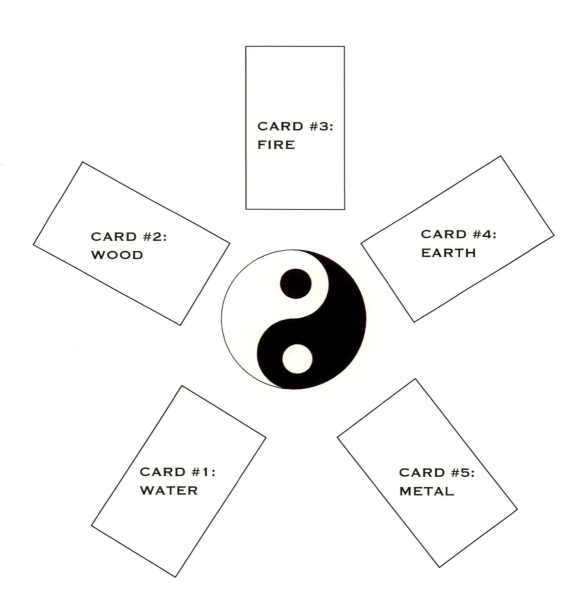

GOAL #2 TAROT NOTES

CARD #1 (WATER):

CARD #2 (WOOD):

CARD #3 (FIRE):

CARD #4 (EARTH):

CARD #5 (METAL):

ADDITIONAL NOTES:

GOAL #3
FIVE ELEMENTS TAROT SPREAD

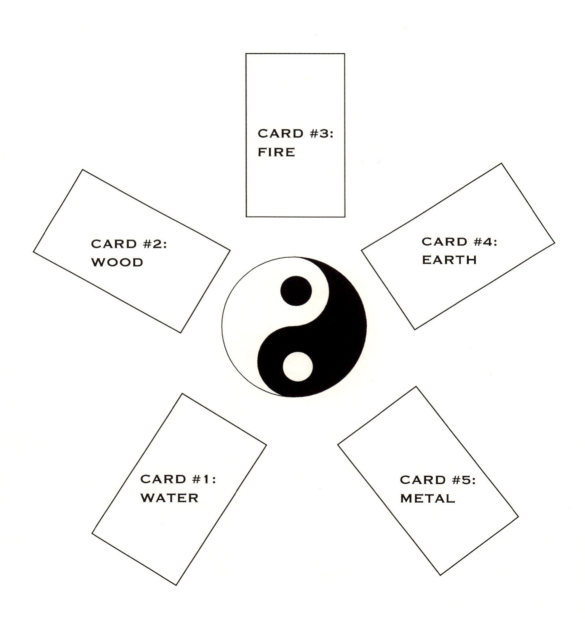

GOAL #3 TAROT NOTES

CARD #1 (WATER):

CARD #2 (WOOD):

CARD #3 (FIRE):

CARD #4 (EARTH):

CARD #5 (METAL):

ADDITIONAL NOTES:

WATER
THE DREAM

WATER ELEMENT PROFILE RANKING: _____

- ○ I need *more* of the Water Element
- ○ I need *less* of the Water Element
- ○ I am balanced in the Water Element

INSIGHTS ABOUT WATER ELEMENT IN MY GOAL

WATER ELEMENT ACTIVITY TRACKER

Activity						
Swimming	○	○	○	○	○	○
Meditation	○	○	○	○	○	○
Restorative Yoga	○	○	○	○	○	○
Painting	○	○	○	○	○	○
Vision Boarding	○	○	○	○	○	○
Social Media break	○	○	○	○	○	○
Breathwork	○	○	○	○	○	○
Sleeping/Napping	○	○	○	○	○	○
Channeling	○	○	○	○	○	○
Journaling	○	○	○	○	○	○

WRITE GOAL #1 AS A DREAM OR IDEA

MY DREAM OR IDEA IS TO/FOR:

_____
_____
_____
_____
_____
_____
_____
_____

I WANT TO CREATE:

_____
_____
_____
_____

BECAUSE I FEEL PASSIONATE ABOUT:

_____
_____
_____
_____
_____

BECAUSE OF MY PERSONAL EXPERIENCE WITH:

_____

_____

_____

_____

_____

AS A RESULT OF MY EXPERIENCE, I LEARNED OR REALIZED:

_____

_____

_____

_____

_____

_____

_____

AND NOW I WANT TO:

_____

_____

_____

_____

_____

_____

I WANT TO MAKE A DIFFERENCE BY:

_____
_____
_____
_____
_____
_____
_____
_____
_____
_____
_____
_____

I CAN SEE MYSELF:

_____
_____
_____
_____
_____
_____
_____
_____
_____

ADDITIONAL NOTES FOR YOUR IDEA OR DREAM:

_____
_____
_____
_____
_____
_____
_____
_____
_____
_____
_____

SKETCHES/DRAWINGS FOR YOUR DREAM:

WHEN YOU ONCE GET AN IDEA IN WHICH YOU BELIEVE WITH ALL YOUR HEART, WORK IT OUT. - HENRY FORD

WRITE GOAL #2 AS A DREAM OR IDEA

MY DREAM OR IDEA IS TO/FOR:
_____
_____
_____
_____
_____
_____
_____
_____
_____

I WANT TO CREATE:
_____
_____
_____
_____

BECAUSE I FEEL PASSIONATE ABOUT:
_____
_____
_____
_____
_____

BECAUSE OF MY PERSONAL EXPERIENCE WITH:

_____
_____
_____
_____
_____
_____

AS A RESULT OF MY EXPERIENCE, I LEARNED OR REALIZED:

_____
_____
_____
_____
_____
_____
_____
_____

AND NOW I WANT TO:

_____
_____
_____
_____
_____
_____

I WANT TO MAKE A DIFFERENCE BY:

_____
_____
_____
_____
_____
_____
_____
_____
_____
_____
_____
_____
_____

I CAN SEE MYSELF:

_____
_____
_____
_____
_____
_____
_____
_____

ADDITIONAL NOTES FOR YOUR IDEA OR DREAM:

_____
_____
_____
_____
_____
_____
_____
_____
_____
_____

SKETCHES/DRAWINGS FOR YOUR DREAM:

WHEN YOU ONCE GET AN IDEA IN WHICH YOU BELIEVE WITH ALL YOUR HEART, WORK IT OUT. - HENRY FORD

WRITE GOAL #3 AS A DREAM OR IDEA

MY DREAM OR IDEA IS TO/FOR:
_____
_____
_____
_____
_____
_____
_____
_____
_____

I WANT TO CREATE:
_____
_____
_____
_____

BECAUSE I FEEL PASSIONATE ABOUT:
_____
_____
_____
_____
_____

BECAUSE OF MY PERSONAL EXPERIENCE WITH:

_____
_____
_____
_____
_____
_____

AS A RESULT OF MY EXPERIENCE, I LEARNED OR REALIZED:

_____
_____
_____
_____
_____
_____

AND NOW I WANT TO:

_____
_____
_____
_____
_____
_____
_____

I WANT TO MAKE A DIFFERENCE BY:
_____
_____
_____
_____
_____
_____
_____
_____
_____
_____
_____
_____

I CAN SEE MYSELF:
_____
_____
_____
_____
_____
_____
_____
_____

ADDITIONAL NOTES FOR YOUR IDEA OR DREAM:

_____
_____
_____
_____
_____
_____
_____
_____
_____
_____

SKETCHES/DRAWINGS FOR YOUR DREAM:

WHEN YOU ONCE GET AN IDEA IN WHICH YOU BELIEVE WITH ALL YOUR HEART, WORK IT OUT. - HENRY FORD

WOOD
THE PLAN

WOOD ELEMENT PROFILE RANKING: _____

○   I need *more* of the Wood Element

○   I need *less* of the Wood Element

○   I am balanced in the Wood Element

INSIGHTS ABOUT WOOD ELEMENT IN MY GOAL

WOOD ELEMENT ACTIVITY TRACKER

Activity							
Walking	○	○	○	○	○	○	○
Hiking	○	○	○	○	○	○	○
Yoga	○	○	○	○	○	○	○
Skiing	○	○	○	○	○	○	○
Active Water Sports	○	○	○	○	○	○	○
Weight Training	○	○	○	○	○	○	○
Writing	○	○	○	○	○	○	○
Driving	○	○	○	○	○	○	○
Traveling	○	○	○	○	○	○	○
Sketching	○	○	○	○	○	○	○

WRITE YOUR PLAN FOR GOAL #1

MY PLAN WILL TAKE THE FORM OF (I.E. BUSINESS PLAN, BOOK
OUTLINE, NOTES, BLUEPRINT, PROTOTYPE):

I WILL CREATE A PLAN THAT INCLUDES:

FOLLOWED BY:

_____
_____
_____
_____
_____
_____
_____
_____
_____
_____
_____
_____
_____
_____
_____
_____
_____

WITH A COMPLETION OF THE PLAN BY:

_____
_____
_____

ADDITIONAL NOTES FOR PLAN:

_____
_____
_____
_____
_____
_____
_____
_____
_____
_____
_____
_____

SKETCHES/DRAWINGS FOR PLAN:

DO NOT FEAR GOING FORWARD SLOWLY; FEAR ONLY TO STAND STILL. - CHINESE PROVERB

WRITE YOUR PLAN FOR GOAL #2

MY PLAN WILL TAKE THE FORM OF (I.E. BUSINESS PLAN, BOOK
OUTLINE, NOTES, BLUEPRINT, PROTOTYPE):

_____

_____

_____

_____

_____

_____

_____

I WILL CREATE A PLAN THAT INCLUDES:

_____

_____

_____

_____

_____

_____

_____

_____

_____

_____

_____

FOLLOWED BY:

_____
_____
_____
_____
_____
_____
_____
_____
_____
_____
_____
_____
_____
_____
_____
_____
_____
_____

WITH A COMPLETION OF THE PLAN BY:

_____
_____
_____

ADDITIONAL NOTES FOR PLAN:

_____
_____
_____
_____
_____
_____
_____
_____
_____
_____
_____
_____

SKETCHES/DRAWINGS FOR PLAN:

DO NOT FEAR GOING FORWARD SLOWLY; FEAR ONLY TO STAND STILL.
- CHINESE PROVERB

WRITE YOUR PLAN FOR GOAL #3

MY PLAN WILL TAKE THE FORM OF (I.E. BUSINESS PLAN, BOOK
OUTLINE, NOTES, BLUEPRINT, PROTOTYPE):

I WILL CREATE A PLAN THAT INCLUDES:

FOLLOWED BY:

_____
_____
_____
_____
_____
_____
_____
_____
_____
_____
_____
_____
_____
_____

WITH A COMPLETION OF THE PLAN BY:

_____
_____
_____

ADDITIONAL NOTES FOR PLAN:

SKETCHES/DRAWINGS FOR PLAN:

DO NOT FEAR GOING FORWARD SLOWLY; FEAR ONLY TO STAND STILL.
-CHINESE PROVERB

FIRE
THE EXECUTION

FIRE ELEMENT PROFILE RANKING: _____

- ○ I need *more* of the Fire Element
- ○ I need *less* of the Fire Element
- ○ I am balanced in the Fire Element

INSIGHTS ABOUT FIRE ELEMENT IN MY GOAL

FIRE ELEMENT ACTIVITY TRACKER

Activity						
Cardio workout	○	○	○	○	○	○
Spinning or cycling	○	○	○	○	○	○
Power Yoga	○	○	○	○	○	○
Socializing	○	○	○	○	○	○
Cross Fit	○	○	○	○	○	○
Acting or Improv	○	○	○	○	○	○
Public Speaking	○	○	○	○	○	○
Horseback Riding	○	○	○	○	○	○
Running	○	○	○	○	○	○

WRITE YOUR EXECUTION FOR GOAL #1

I AM COMMITTED TO MY IDEA/PROJECT AND INTEND TO:

_____
_____
_____
_____
_____
_____
_____
_____

I AM PASSIONATE ABOUT EXECUTING MY IDEA BECAUSE:

_____
_____
_____
_____
_____
_____
_____
_____
_____
_____
_____
_____

I COMMIT TO WORKING ON THIS PROJECT/GOAL FOR _____ HOURS PER WEEK FOR _____ MONTHS IN ORDER TO FINISH. (PROVIDE DETAILS OF HOW AND WHEN YOU WILL EXECUTE YOUR PLAN, I.E. DAYS OF THE WEEK, HOURS, ETC.):

_____
_____
_____
_____
_____
_____
_____
_____
_____
_____
_____
_____
_____
_____
_____

I INTEND IS TO FINISH THE FIRST PHASE OF MY GOAL/PROJECT BY:

_____
_____
_____
_____

ADDITIONAL NOTES FOR PROJECT/GOAL:

SKETCHES/DRAWINGS FOR PROJECT/GOAL:

WHAT MATTERS MOST IS HOW WELL YOU WALK THROUGH THE FIRE
- CHARLES BUKOWSKI

WRITE YOUR EXECUTION FOR GOAL #2

I AM COMMITTED TO MY IDEA/PROJECT AND INTEND TO:
_____
_____
_____
_____
_____
_____
_____
_____

I AM PASSIONATE ABOUT EXECUTING MY IDEA BECAUSE:
_____
_____
_____
_____
_____
_____
_____
_____
_____
_____

I COMMIT TO WORKING ON THIS PROJECT/GOAL FOR _____ HOURS PER WEEK FOR _____ MONTHS IN ORDER TO FINISH. (PROVIDE DETAILS OF HOW AND WHEN YOU WILL EXECUTE YOUR PLAN, I.E. DAYS OF THE WEEK, HOURS, ETC.):

_____
_____
_____
_____
_____
_____
_____
_____
_____
_____
_____
_____
_____
_____
_____
_____

I INTEND IS TO FINISH THE FIRST PHASE OF MY GOAL/PROJECT BY:

_____
_____
_____
_____

ADDITIONAL NOTES FOR PROJECT/GOAL:

_____
_____
_____
_____
_____
_____
_____
_____
_____
_____

SKETCHES/DRAWINGS FOR PROJECT/GOAL:

WHAT MATTERS MOST IS HOW WELL YOU WALK THROUGH THE FIRE
- CHARLES BUKOWSKI

WRITE YOUR EXECUTION FOR GOAL #3

I AM COMMITTED TO MY IDEA/PROJECT AND INTEND TO:

_____
_____
_____
_____
_____
_____
_____
_____

I AM PASSIONATE ABOUT EXECUTING MY IDEA BECAUSE:

_____
_____
_____
_____
_____
_____
_____
_____
_____
_____
_____

I COMMIT TO WORKING ON THIS PROJECT/GOAL FOR _____ HOURS PER WEEK FOR _____ MONTHS IN ORDER TO FINISH. (PROVIDE DETAILS OF HOW AND WHEN YOU WILL EXECUTE YOUR PLAN, I.E. DAYS OF THE WEEK, HOURS, ETC.):

_____
_____
_____
_____
_____
_____
_____
_____
_____
_____
_____
_____
_____
_____
_____
_____

I INTEND IS TO FINISH THE FIRST PHASE OF MY GOAL/PROJECT BY:

_____
_____
_____
_____

ADDITIONAL NOTES FOR PROJECT/GOAL:

_____
_____
_____
_____
_____
_____
_____
_____
_____
_____

SKETCHES/DRAWINGS FOR PROJECT/GOAL:

WHAT MATTERS MOST IS HOW WELL YOU WALK THROUGH THE FIRE
- CHARLES BUKOWSKI

EARTH
THE RECEPTIVE

EARTH ELEMENT PROFILE RANKING: _____

- ○ I need *more* of the Earth Element

- ○ I need *less* of the Earth Element

- ○ I am balanced in the Earth Element

INSIGHTS ABOUT EARTH ELEMENT IN MY GOAL

EARTH ELEMENT ACTIVITY TRACKER

Activity							
Gardening	○	○	○	○	○	○	○
Nature Walks	○	○	○	○	○	○	○
Pottery	○	○	○	○	○	○	○
Cooking/Baking	○	○	○	○	○	○	○
Breadmaking	○	○	○	○	○	○	○
Crafting	○	○	○	○	○	○	○
Hosting People	○	○	○	○	○	○	○
Camping	○	○	○	○	○	○	○
Resting	○	○	○	○	○	○	○

WRITE HOW YOUR GOAL #1 WILL IMPACT OTHERS

I WANT TO HELP:

_____
_____
_____
_____
_____
_____
_____
_____

MY IDEA WILL PROVIDE A SOLUTION FOR:

_____
_____
_____
_____
_____
_____
_____
_____
_____
_____
_____

I WILL REACH MY IDEAL [CUSTOMER/AUDIENCE/PERSON] THROUGH [MARKETING/SOCIAL MEDIA/REACHING OUT/ETC.]:

_____
_____
_____
_____
_____
_____
_____
_____

FOR THE SUCCESS OF MY GOAL, I WANT TO ATTRACT:

_____
_____
_____
_____
_____
_____
_____
_____
_____
_____
_____
_____

ADDITIONAL NOTES FOR PROJECT/GOAL:

_____
_____
_____
_____
_____
_____
_____
_____

SKETCHES/DRAWINGS FOR PROJECT/GOAL:

LISTEN, ARE YOU BREATHING JUST A LITTLE, AND CALLING IT A LIFE?
- MARY OLIVER

WRITE HOW YOUR GOAL #2 WILL IMPACT OTHERS

I WANT TO HELP:
_____
_____
_____
_____
_____
_____
_____
_____

MY IDEA WILL PROVIDE A SOLUTION FOR:
_____
_____
_____
_____
_____
_____
_____
_____
_____
_____

I WILL REACH MY IDEAL [CUSTOMER/AUDIENCE/PERSON] THROUGH [MARKETING/SOCIAL MEDIA/REACHING OUT/ETC.]:

_____
_____
_____
_____
_____
_____
_____
_____

FOR THE SUCCESS OF MY GOAL, I WANT TO ATTRACT:

_____
_____
_____
_____
_____
_____
_____
_____
_____
_____
_____
_____

ADDITIONAL NOTES FOR PROJECT/GOAL:

_____
_____
_____
_____
_____
_____
_____
_____

SKETCHES/DRAWINGS FOR PROJECT/GOAL:

LISTEN, ARE YOU BREATHING JUST A LITTLE, AND CALLING IT A LIFE?
- MARY OLIVER

WRITE HOW YOUR GOAL #3 WILL IMPACT OTHERS

I WANT TO HELP:

_____
_____
_____
_____
_____
_____
_____
_____

MY IDEA WILL PROVIDE A SOLUTION FOR:

_____
_____
_____
_____
_____
_____
_____
_____

I WILL REACH MY IDEAL [CUSTOMER/AUDIENCE/PERSON] THROUGH [MARKETING/SOCIAL MEDIA/REACHING OUT/ETC.]:

_____
_____
_____
_____
_____
_____
_____
_____

FOR THE SUCCESS OF MY GOAL, I WANT TO ATTRACT:

_____
_____
_____
_____
_____
_____
_____
_____
_____
_____
_____

ADDITIONAL NOTES FOR PROJECT/GOAL:

_____
_____
_____
_____
_____
_____
_____
_____
_____

SKETCHES/DRAWINGS FOR PROJECT/GOAL:

LISTEN, ARE YOU BREATHING JUST A LITTLE, AND CALLING IT A LIFE?
- MARY OLIVER

METAL
THE ADJUSTMENTS

METAL ELEMENT PROFILE RANKING: _____

- ○ I need *more* of the Metal Element
- ○ I need *less* of the Metal Element
- ○ I am balanced in the Metal Element

INSIGHTS ABOUT METAL ELEMENT IN MY GOAL

METAL ELEMENT ACTIVITY TRACKER

Activity							
Organizing	○	○	○	○	○	○	○
Decluttering	○	○	○	○	○	○	○
Cleaning	○	○	○	○	○	○	○
Technical Drawing	○	○	○	○	○	○	○
Book Editing	○	○	○	○	○	○	○
Framing photos	○	○	○	○	○	○	○
Photo/video Editing	○	○	○	○	○	○	○
Playing Piano	○	○	○	○	○	○	○
Landscaping	○	○	○	○	○	○	○

WHAT CHANGES DO I NEED TO MAKE FROM MY ORIGINAL GOAL #1, IF ANY?

I NEED TO ELIMINATE OR PARE DOWN:
_____
_____
_____
_____
_____
_____
_____
_____
_____

I NEED TO CHANGE:
_____
_____
_____
_____
_____
_____
_____
_____
_____
_____
_____

I CAN IMPROVE UPON _____ BY TAKING OUT/CHANGING/ADDING:

_____

_____

_____

_____

_____

_____

_____

I NEED TO GO BACK TO THE _____ PHASE IN ORDER TO:

_____

_____

_____

_____

_____

_____

_____

_____

_____

_____

_____

ADDITIONAL NOTES FOR PROJECT/GOAL:

SKETCHES/DRAWINGS FOR PROJECT/GOAL:

THE DETAILS ARE NOT THE DETAILS. THEY MAKE THE DESIGN.
- CHARLES EAMES

WHAT CHANGES DO I NEED TO MAKE FROM MY ORIGINAL GOAL #2, IF ANY?

I NEED TO ELIMINATE OR PARE DOWN:

_____

_____

_____

_____

_____

_____

_____

_____

I NEED TO CHANGE:

_____

_____

_____

_____

_____

_____

_____

_____

_____

_____

I CAN IMPROVE UPON _____ BY TAKING OUT/CHANGING/ADDING:

_____

_____

_____

_____

_____

_____

_____

I NEED TO GO BACK TO THE _____ PHASE IN ORDER TO:

_____

_____

_____

_____

_____

_____

_____

_____

_____

_____

_____

ADDITIONAL NOTES FOR PROJECT/GOAL:

SKETCHES/DRAWINGS FOR PROJECT/GOAL:

THE DETAILS ARE NOT THE DETAILS. THEY MAKE THE DESIGN.
- CHARLES EAMES

WHAT CHANGES DO I NEED TO MAKE FROM MY ORIGINAL GOAL #3, IF ANY?

I NEED TO ELIMINATE OR PARE DOWN:
_____
_____
_____
_____
_____
_____
_____
_____

I NEED TO CHANGE:
_____
_____
_____
_____
_____
_____
_____
_____
_____
_____

I CAN IMPROVE UPON _____ BY TAKING OUT/CHANGING/ADDING:

_____
_____
_____
_____
_____
_____
_____

I NEED TO GO BACK TO THE _____ PHASE IN ORDER TO:

_____
_____
_____
_____
_____
_____
_____
_____
_____
_____
_____
_____

ADDITIONAL NOTES FOR PROJECT/GOAL:

SKETCHES/DRAWINGS FOR PROJECT/GOAL:

THE DETAILS ARE NOT THE DETAILS. THEY MAKE THE DESIGN.
- CHARLES EAMES

SLEEP

PEACEFULLY

DREAM

SWEETLY

MANIFEST

ABUNDANTLY

ABOUT THE AUTHOR

Tisha is an entertainment attorney and the author of Missing Element, Hidden Strength, along with four other books.

Tisha holds a degree in law, economics, and interior design with certifications in yoga, feng shui, and coaching. Tisha advises and represents clients using her entrepreneurial experience, legal and publishing expertise, and practical wisdom to help clients realize their potentials and strategize for optimal success.

When not practicing law, Tisha lives in Ojai, CA with her wife, poodle, step-cat, and works on becoming a legal thriller novelist.

For more information, visit Tisha at www.tishamorris.com.

Made in United States
Orlando, FL
11 June 2023